DOCTOR · WHO

ACTIVITY COLLECTION
CONTENTS

COPY AND COLOUR THE DOCTOR

CAREFULLY COPY EACH HEXAGON FROM THE SMALLER GRID INTO THE LARGER GRID TO DRAW YOUR OWN PICTURE OF THE DOCTOR.

⬡ COMPLETE THE QUOTE

CHOOSE WORDS FROM THE BOX AT THE BOTTOM OF
THE PAGE TO COMPLETE THESE QUOTES.

1. "You're just skin, Cassandra. _____
   and skin!" — *Rose*

2. "You are not _____" — *The Face of Boe*

3. "We are Human Point Two. Every citizen will receive
   a free _____. You will become like us." — *Cyberman*

4. "This is not war. This is _____ _____." - *Dalek*

5. "I went to the _____ today." — *Martha*

6. "My home planet is far away and long since gone.
   But its name lives on. _____." — *The Doctor*

7. "A lord is trained from the day he is born to behave
   like a lord, but there is something _____
   about you." - *Shakespeare*

UPGRADE

ALONE

PEST

MOON

CONTROL

LIPSTICK

DIFFERENT

GALLIFREY

DALEK DASH

FOUR DALEKS ARE CHASING THE DOCTOR. ADD UP THE NUMBERS IN EACH PATH TO SEE WHICH DALEK WILL REACH HIM FIRST. THE SMALLEST NUMBER IS THE FASTEST DALEK.

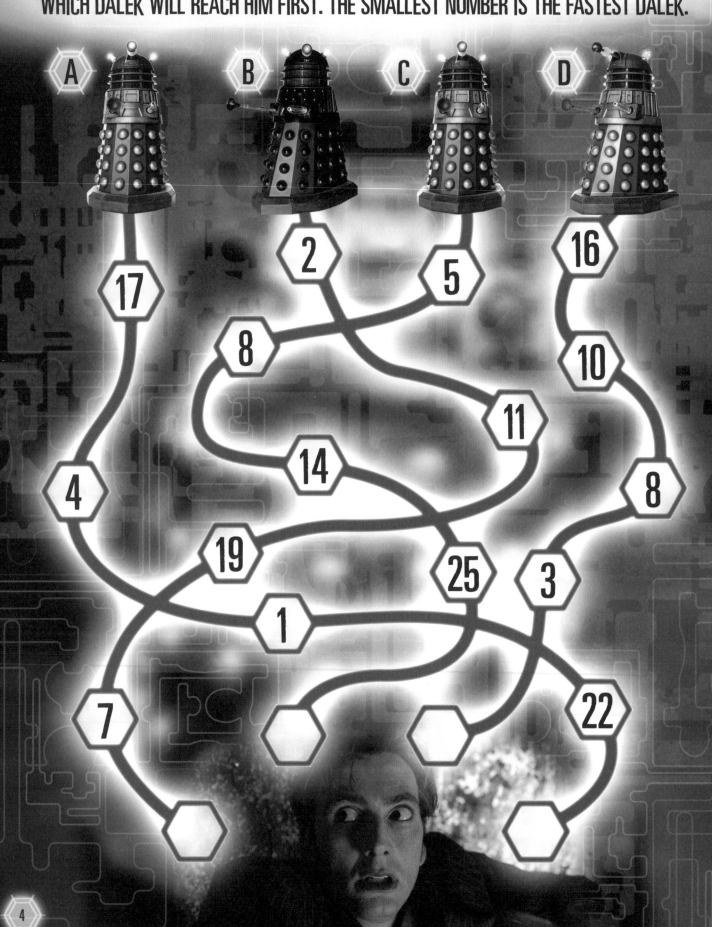

 # JUDOON JIGSAW

LOOK AT THE MISSING PIECES IN THIS PICTURE OF THE JUDOON. WHICH OF THE SHAPES BELOW WOULD COMPLETE THE PICTURE?

WORD WHEEL

ANSWER THE QUESTIONS TO FILL IN THE WORDS AROUND THE WHEEL. THE LAST LETTER OF EACH WORD IS THE FIRST LETTER OF THE NEXT.

1. Professor who created the Genetic Manipulation Device.

2. Aliens who took over the British Government.

3. Nurse protecting the Face of Boe.

4. The leader of the Racnoss.

5. Financer and girlfriend of the Professor in clue 1.

6. Form of magic used by Lilith, Bloodtide and Doomfinger.

7. Institute that owned H.C. Clements.

8. Creature from Skaro.

9. Aliens who pretended to be teachers.

10. The Racnoss look like this insect.

CHAMELEON CIRCUIT

THE TARDIS' CHAMELEON CIRCUIT ALLOWS IT TO CHANGE
THE WAY IT LOOKS, TO BLEND IN TO WHEREVER IT LANDS.
UNFORTUNATELY, IT'S BEEN BROKEN FOR YEARS! IF IT WAS
WORKING, WHAT WOULD YOU DISGUISE THE TARDIS AS
WHEN IT LANDS ON EARTH? DRAW IT IN BELOW.

SONIC PANIC

THE DOCTOR HAS PUT HIS SONIC SCREWDRIVER DOWN SOMEWHERE AND NOW HE CAN'T FIND IT. CAN YOU SEE IT IN THE PICTURE?

MARTHA'S MESSAGE

MARTHA HAS LEFT THE DOCTOR A CODED MESSAGE. DO THE SUMS BELOW TO WORK OUT WHAT SHE IS SAYING.

8x2=   27-12=   5+11=   7+9=   3+2=   13-9=

__   __   __   __   __   __

3x5=   12+9=   6+14=   5x4=   18-3=

__   __   __   __   __

16+3=   7-2=   1+4=   10+3=   3x7=   7+6=   .

__   __   __   __   __   __ .

1+1=   7-6=   2+1=   5+6=   10-1=   7x2=

__   __   __   __   __   __

8-7=   9+5=   2x4=   5x3=   19+2=   21-3=   .

__   __   __   __ .

1 = A
2 = B
3 = C
4 = D
5 = E
6 = F
7 = G
8 = H
9 = I
10 = J
11 = K
12 = L
13 = M
14 = N
15 = O
16 = P
17 = Q
18 = R
19 = S
20 = T
21 = U
22 = V
23 = W
24 = X
25 = Y
26 = Z

TARDIS MIX-UP

THE DOCTOR HAS LANDED IN THE 1950S, NEXT TO A REAL POLICE BOX, AND NOW HE'S NOT SURE WHICH IS HIS! CAN YOU FIND FIVE DIFFERENCES BETWEEN THEM AND WORK OUT WHICH IS THE TARDIS?

WHO'S NEXT?

WORK OUT THE PATTERNS IN THE SETS OF IMAGES BELOW, THEN PICK FROM THE BOX AT THE BOTTOM WHICH YOU THINK SHOULD COME NEXT EACH TIME.

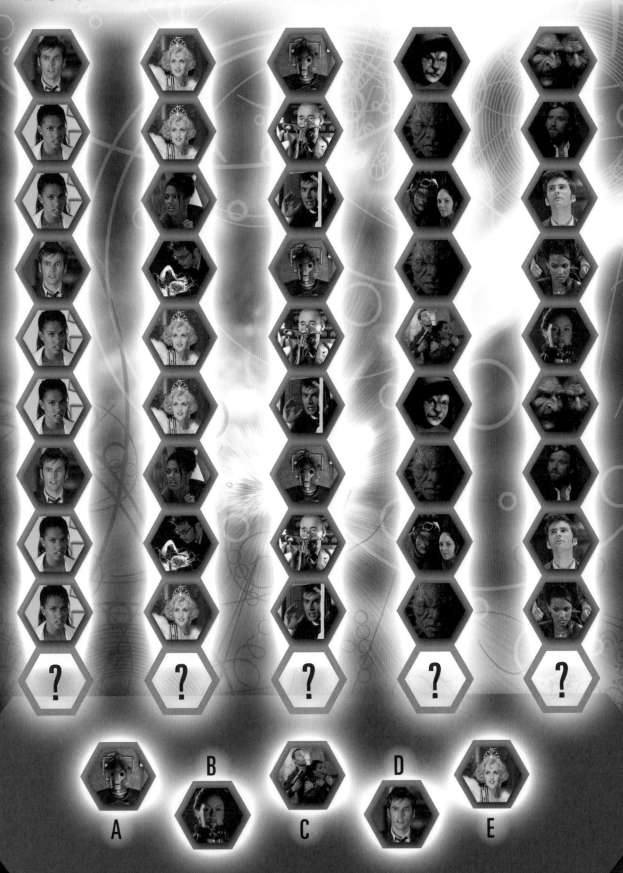

WHERE ON EARTH ARE WE?

LOOK AT THE SETS OF CLUES BELOW AND SEE IF YOU CAN WORK OUT WHERE THE TARDIS HAS LANDED THIS TIME.

A

Some of the buildings are like giant triangles.

It's very hot and sandy.

There's a huge stone statue that looks like a cat.

_____

B

The traffic is very busy and there are lots of yellow taxis.

The buildings here are very tall.

There's a statue of a lady holding a flaming torch.

_____

C

It's the world's second longest river.

There's rainforest all around.

And some really strange animals!

_____

OOD SQUARES

HELP THE DOCTOR ROUND UP THE OOD BY PLAYING THIS GAME WITH A FRIEND.

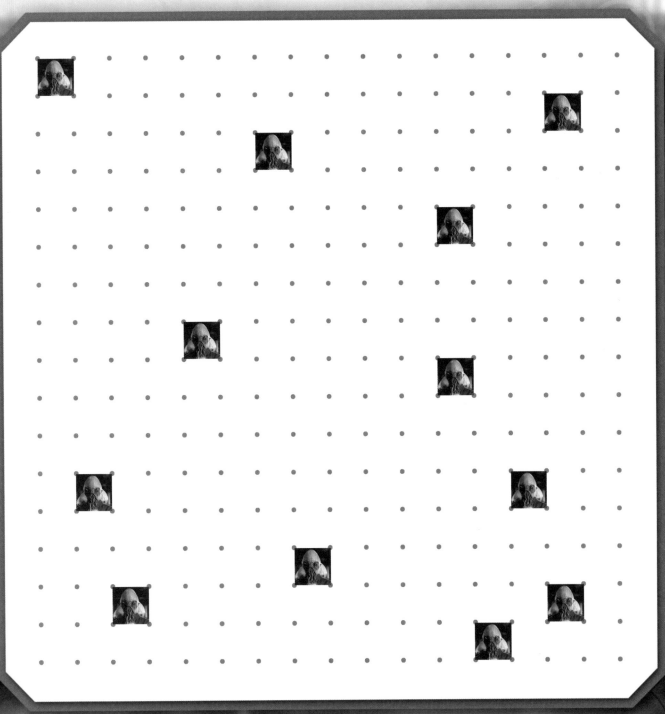

HOW TO PLAY

Take turns drawing a line between two dots. Every time you form a square, write your initials in it. Try and collect as many squares as possible containing an Ood. The winner is the player who manages to collect the most Ood.

FOLLOW THAT CAR

A ROBOT SANTA TAXI DRIVER HAS KIDNAPPED DONNA.
LEAD THE TARDIS THROUGH THE MAZE TO RESCUE HER.

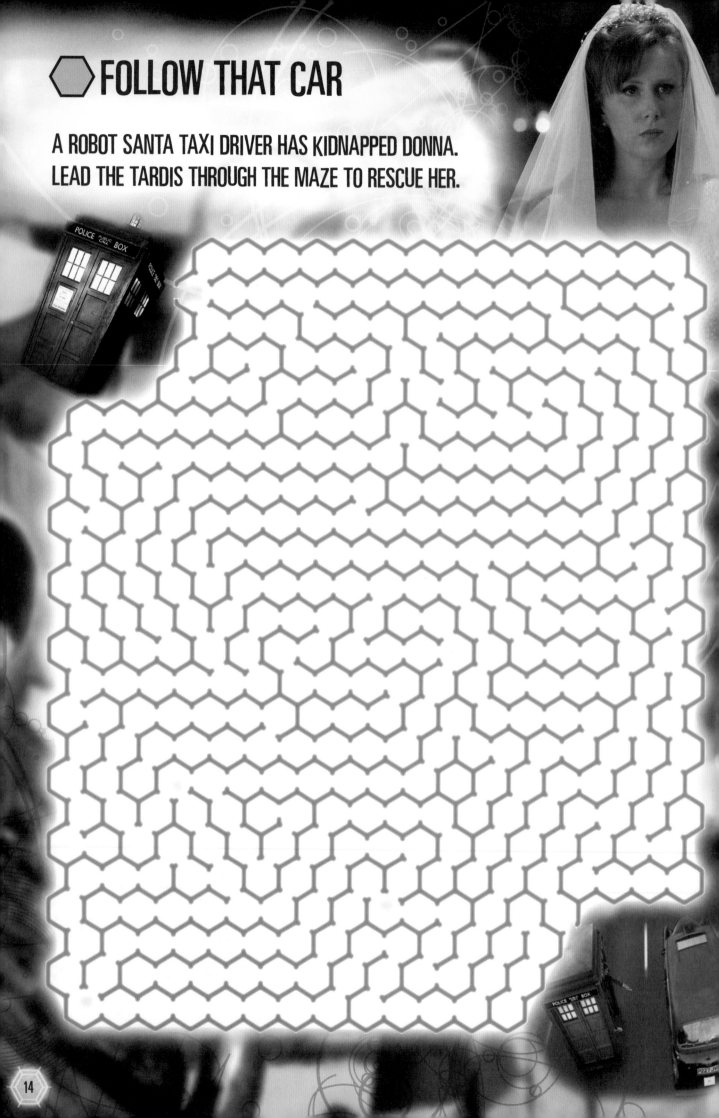

LOST LOCATIONS

LOOK AT THE WORDSEARCH BELOW AND SEE IF YOU CAN FIND
SOME OF THE PLACES THE DOCTOR HAS TRAVELLED TO.

```
D W D G P G O H B R Q W T
X C T Y U I A L L R K L O
C A N A R Y W H A R F O T
A H G V C E M N C D S N A
R F Y U C X V G K I P D E
D I O N J M A S H Y U O N
I X A K R O P T O R F N T
F R U J M O P L L N H G T
F R T Y S N E W E A R T H
```

LONDON

NEW EARTH

MOON

KROP TOR

CARDIFF

CANARY WHARF

BLACK HOLE

FRANCE

15

TWO OF A KIND JUDOON

ONLY TWO OF THESE PICTURES OF THE JUDOON ARE THE SAME. CAN YOU FIND THEM?

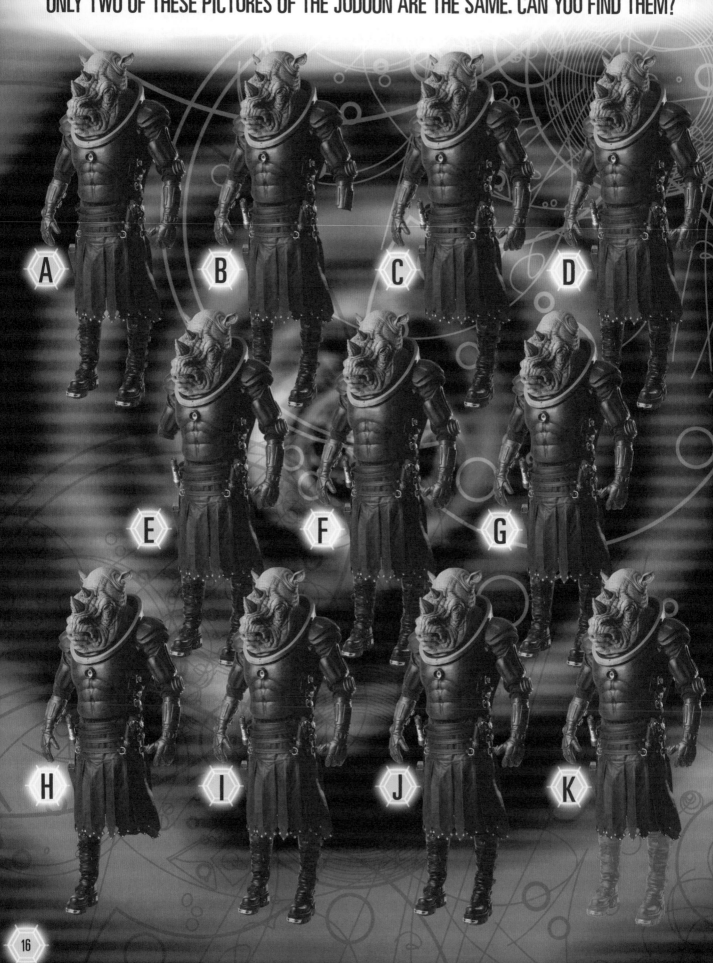

DISGUISE TIME

THE DOCTOR AND MARTHA HAVE LANDED IN ANCIENT ROME. DRAW THEM SOME NEW CLOTHES SO THEY DON'T LOOK OUT OF PLACE.

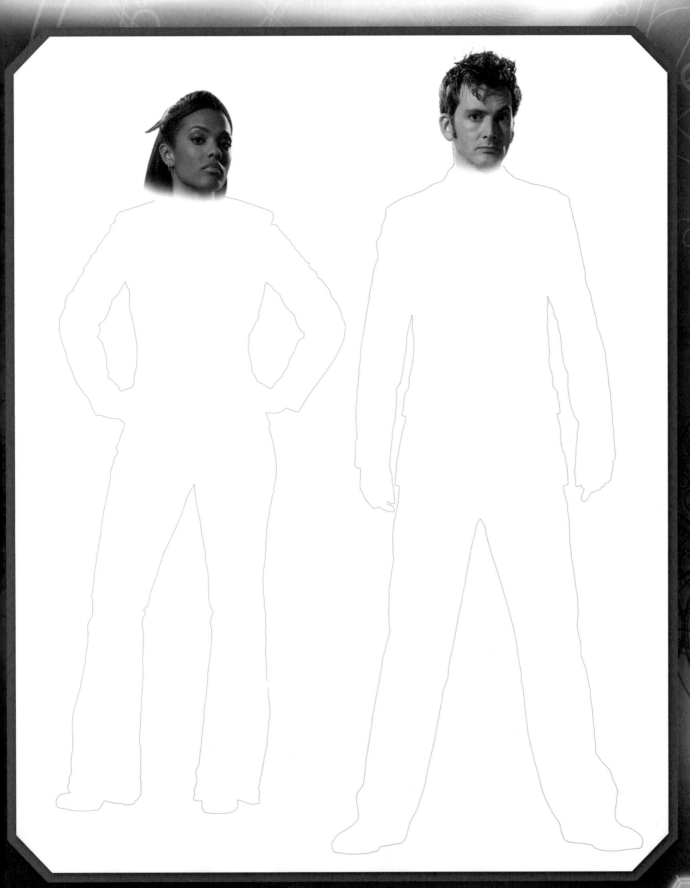

CYBER CANCELLATION CODE

MICKEY HELPED TO DEFEAT THE CYBERMEN BY CRACKING THE CANCELLATION CODE. CIRCLE ALL THE NUMBERS LISTED BELOW IN THE GRID, JUST LIKE IN A WORDSEARCH. READING FROM LEFT TO RIGHT, WRITE THE NUMBERS THAT ARE USED TWICE IN THE ORDER THEY APPEAR IN THE BOXES BELOW, TO REVEAL THE CANCELLATION CODE.

42719   89573   09354   01924   74367

63900   66761   72384   56502

6	3	9	0	0	6	6	5	1	4
6	5	0	2	9	7	4	9	6	3
7	1	2	3	4	5	2	9	8	7
6	8	9	8	9	5	7	3	1	0
1	1	3	2	1	4	1	6	6	7
3	2	3	5	7	0	9	3	5	4
7	4	3	6	7	4	5	5	6	1
9	4	2	5	4	2	1	3	7	9
1	7	4	0	1	9	2	4	2	6
7	6	9	2	4	2	3	2	1	1

CANCELLATION CODE:

◇ MEMORY GAME

SPEND A COUPLE OF MINUTES LOOKING AT THE PICTURE BELOW, THEN TURN THE PAGE AND SEE HOW MANY QUESTIONS YOU CAN ANSWER.

WHAT CAN YOU REMEMBER?

1. How many circles are on the banner in the background?

2. What colour is the carpet?

3. How many steps up is the Doctor standing?

4. What is Martha doing in the picture?

5. What is the Doctor doing with his hands?

WORD GRID

FIT THE WORDS BELOW INTO THE GRID. THE LETTERS IN THE YELLOW BOXES CAN BE REARRANGED TO MAKE A WORD WHICH RELATES TO ALL THE OTHER WORDS.

OOD

CAPTAIN JACK

DALEKS

CYBERMEN

SIR ROBERT MACLEISH

WEREWOLF

DOCTOR

SYCORAX

THE RELATED WORD IS

___ ___ ___ ___ ___ ___ ___ ___

HISTORY LESSON

THE DOCTOR HAS TRAVELLED ALL THROUGH TIME. IMAGINE YOU'RE READING A HISTORY BOOK AND SUDDENLY YOU COME ACROSS A PICTURE OF THE DOCTOR! WRITE ABOUT THE TIME HE IS IN AND DRAW A PICTURE TO GO WITH IT.

DODGY DALEK

ONE OF THESE DALEKS ISN'T REAL. CAN YOU SPOT THE
ONE THAT IS DIFFERENT TO THE OTHERS?

A

B

C

D

E

F

FAMILY TIES

WHICH LINE CONNECTS MARTHA TO THESE MEMBERS OF HER FAMILY? FOLLOW A, B AND C TO FIND OUT.

A

B

C

TISH

LEO

MUM

WHICH BIT FITS?

LOOK AT THE MISSING BITS OF THE IMAGE BELOW. WHICH OF THE SHAPES BELOW WOULD COMPLETE THE PICTURE?

TALK TO THE FACE

THE FACE OF BOE HAS
A MESSAGE FOR THE
DOCTOR. FOLLOW THE
INSTRUCTIONS BELOW TO
WORK OUT WHAT IT IS.

	A	B	C	D
1	why	Martha	you	New Earth
2	are	Krop Tor	Cybermen	Tish
3	Francine	to	how	Rose
4	Captain Jack	not	Leo	hi
5	Daleks	Sarah Jane	at	alone

TAKE AWAY...

- the words that could be a question.
- names of the Doctor's companions.
- names of planets.
- metal monsters.
- anyone in Martha's family.
- words with only two letters.

COPY AND COLOUR OOD

CAREFULLY COPY EACH HEXAGON FROM THE SMALLER GRID INTO THE LARGER GRID TO DRAW YOUR OWN PICTURE OF AN OOD.

CREATE A CODE WHEEL

IF YOU WANT TO LEAVE A MESSAGE FOR THE DOCTOR (OR YOUR FRIENDS), IT'S BEST TO PUT IT IN CODE TO PREVENT ANY ALIEN IMPOSTERS (OR YOUR MUM) PICKING IT UP! FOLLOW THE INSTRUCTIONS TO CREATE YOUR OWN CODE WHEEL, THEN SEE IF YOU CAN CRACK THE CODES BELOW WITH IT.

1. Cut out the two circles on the opposite page. If you don't want to cut up your book, trace or copy them on to a sheet of paper or card, and cut them out.

2. Place the smaller wheel on top of the bigger wheel, and push a paper fastener through the centres of both. Bend the ends of the fastener outwards to fix the wheels in place.

3. To begin with, line the wheels up so that both As are level. You can now use the wheel to create lots of different shift codes...

4. Try turning the smaller wheel one space to the left, so that the Z on the big wheel lines up with the A on the smaller wheel. To code a message, find the letter you want to use on the big wheel, then write down the letter on the smaller wheel that it corresponds with.

   For example, THE DOCTOR, would be:

   # UIF CNDUPS

5. To decode the message, find the letter on the smaller wheel, and write down the corresponding letter on the bigger wheel.

6. You can turn the wheel as many times to the left or right as you like, to create many different codes, but don't forget to always start with the As together. Let the person you are writing to know what the code is by putting 'L' for left and 'R' for right, and then the number of moves, in brackets before your coded message. Try the ones below for practise!

(L17) SJHWVRR

(R4) HEPIO

(L8) GSBZLS

HOW MANY SONIC SCREWDRIVERS CAN YOU COUNT HERE?

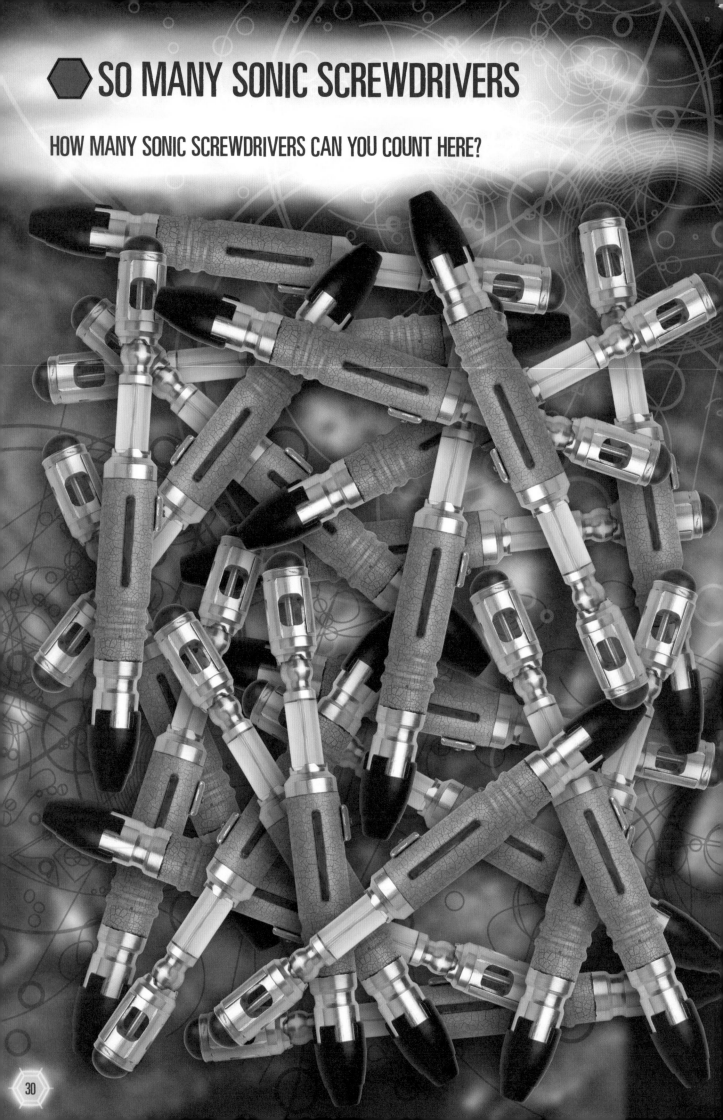

ALL IN THE DETAIL

LOOK CAREFULLY AT THE IMAGES BELOW. CAN YOU GUESS WHICH ALIENS THEY ARE?

GIRL TALK

WHICH OF THE DOCTOR'S FEMALE COMPANIONS SAID THESE THINGS? MATCH THE QUOTES TO THE PICTURES.

"Those Cybermen things, that battle in the sky... I had a cousin, Adeola. She worked at Canary Wharf. Never came home."

"But it's just a box... But it's huge! How does it do that? It's wood!"

"I thought you'd died. I waited for you and when you didn't come back, I thought you must have died."

TO THE RESCUE

MARTHA IS BEING HELD CAPTIVE BY THE DALEKS. ADD UP THE NUMBERS TO HELP THE DOCTOR RESCUE HER. THE SMALLEST NUMBER IS THE SHORTEST PATH.

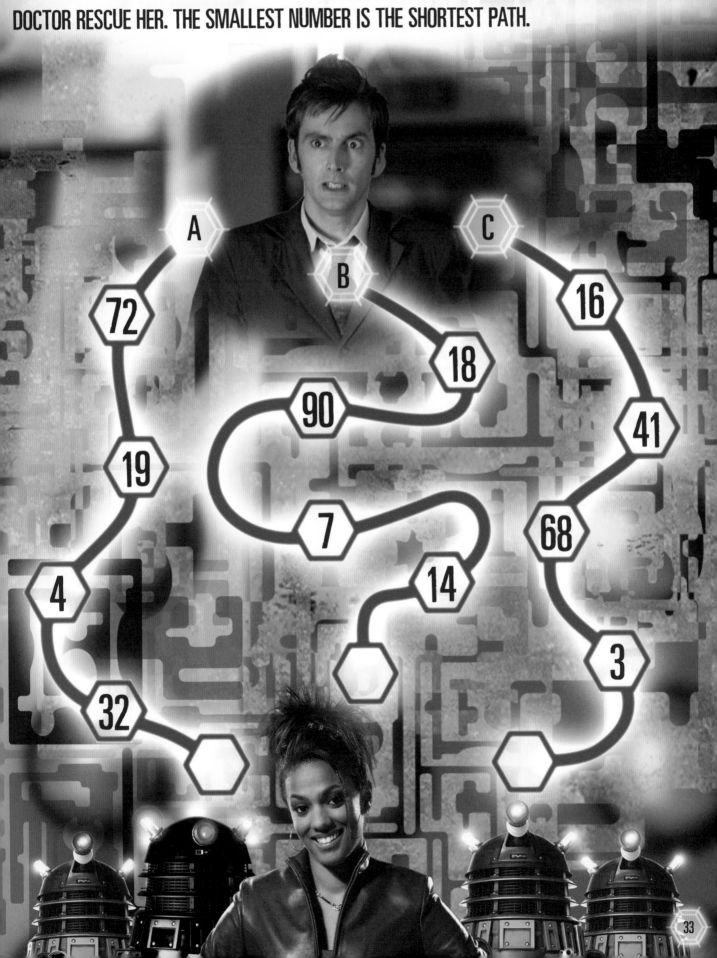

DOCTOR WHOSE?

SOME OF THE ITEMS BELOW BELONG TO THE DOCTOR, AND SOME CERTAINLY DON'T! CIRCLE THE THINGS THAT DO AND CROSS OUT THE THINGS THAT DON'T.

LOST LETTERS

CROSS OUT ALL THE LETTERS BELOW THAT APPEAR TWICE. REARRANGE THE REMAINING LETTERS TO REVEAL SOMETHING THE DOCTOR HAS LOST.

N F P
H U Q G
R S B G
A L Y F
V F J Q
O U L W
G H Y P
B H M N
E F J A
W M J V

_____

ALL IN THE WORD

CHALLENGE A FRIEND TO SEE HOW MANY WORDS YOU CAN EACH MAKE FROM THE WORD BELOW. SET YOURSELVES A TIME LIMIT AND SEE HOW FAR YOU GET. SCORE 1 POINT FOR WORDS UNDER 4 LETTERS LONG, 2 POINTS FOR 4 LETTER WORDS, 3 POINTS FOR 5 LETTER WORDS, 4 POINTS FOR 6 LETTER WORDS AND 5 POINTS FOR ANY WORDS OF 7 OR MORE LETTERS.

RAXACORICOFALLAPATORIOUS

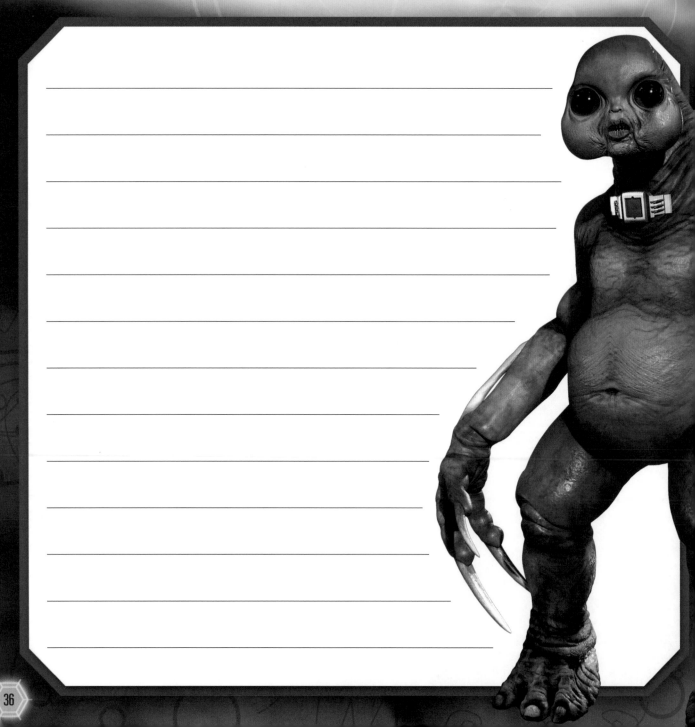

ALIEN TRUE OR FALSE

SOME OF THE ALIEN FACTS BELOW ARE TRUE AND SOME ARE FALSE. READ EACH ONE AND DECIDE WHETHER THEY ARE REAL OR NOT.

1. One of the Carrionites disguised herself as a beautiful woman. — TRUE FALSE

2. The Slitheen used a pig to fly a spaceship into the Thames. — TRUE FALSE

3. Martha first met a Dalek in New York. — TRUE FALSE

4. The Judoon are intergalactic doctors. — TRUE FALSE

5. Mickey stayed on the parallel Earth to fight the Cybermen. — TRUE FALSE

6. Lazarus built a machine that made him able to fly. — TRUE FALSE

7. Plasmavores drink blood. — TRUE FALSE

8. The Racnoss have eight legs. — TRUE FALSE

# CARRIONITE FRIGHT!

CAN YOU SPOT TEN DIFFERENCES BETWEEN THESE TWO SCARY PICTURES OF THE CARRIONITES?

TARDIS MAZE

WITH ALL ITS MANY CORRIDORS AND ROOMS, THE TARDIS REALLY CAN BE LIKE A MAZE TO ANYONE BUT THE DOCTOR! SEE IF YOU CAN FIND YOUR WAY THROUGH THIS TARDIS MAZE.

START

FINISH

SOMETHING ODD ABOUT THE OOD

THERE'S SOMETHING FUNNY ABOUT SOME OF THESE OOD, ONLY ONE OF THEM IS REAL.
WHICH ONE IS IT?

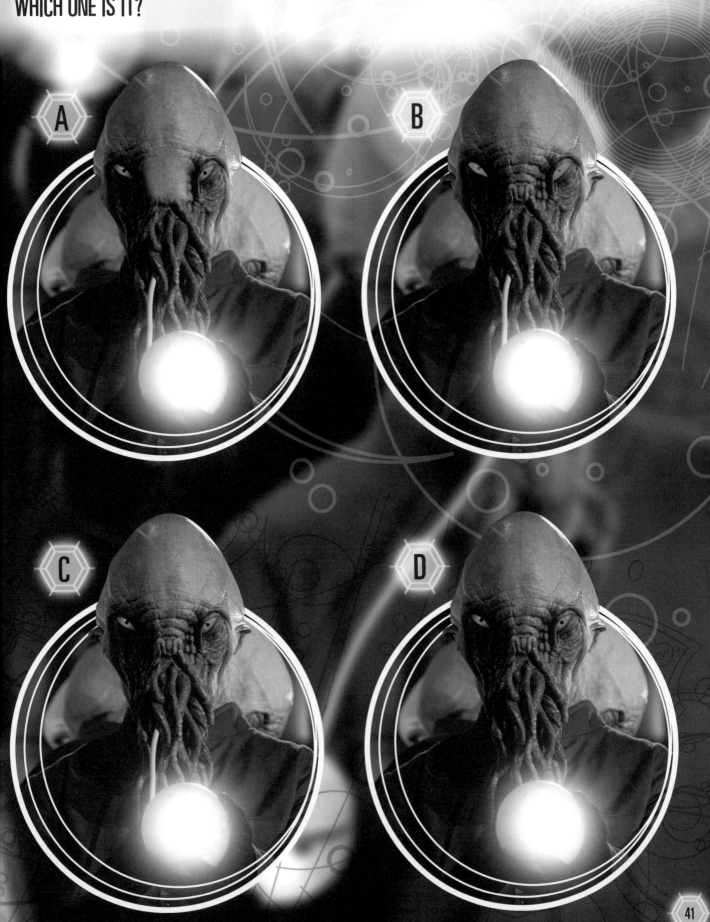

⬡ PUZZLE PIECES

PARTS OF THE PICTURE BELOW ARE MISSING. LOOK AT THE PUZZLE PIECES AND SEE IF YOU CAN WORK OUT WHICH OF THEM FIT IN THE HOLES.

CHIC PAPER

ENTIFICATION CARD TO HELP YOU BLUFF
ITO A TOP SECRET LABORATORY.

⬡ COSMIC QUIZ

TEST YOUR KNOWLEDGE OF THE DOCTOR'S ADVENTURES AND SEE HOW MANY OF THESE
QUESTIONS YOU CAN ANSWER.

1. **What were the names of the Carrionites that used Shakespeare's plays in their magic?**

A. Rose, Martha and Sarah Jane.

B. Bloodtide, Doomfinger and Lilith.

C. Mildred, Hermione and Winnie.

2. **Who had the Plasmavore murdered?**

A. The Child Princess of Padrivole Regency Nine.

B. Blon Fel Fotch Pasameer-Day Slitheen.

C. Mickey Smith.

3. **What was inside the Genesis Ark?**

A. Cybermen.

B. Daleks.

C. Reapers.

4. **Where did the Judoon take the hospital that Martha worked at?**

A. Cardiff.

B. Krop Tor.

C. The Moon.

5. **How do you spell the name of the planet that the Slitheen come from?**

A. Raxacoricofallapatorious.

B. Raxacorickofallapatoryous.

C. Raxacoricophalapatorious.

6. How many Daleks were in the Cult of Skaro?

A. Seven.

B. Three.

C. Four.

7. What was the name of the man who created the Genetic Manipulation Device?

A. Lumic.

B. Lazarus.

C. Icarus.

8. Where do the Macra live?

A. Under the motorway.

B. Under the bed.

C. Under the sea.

9. What do Torchwood say about aliens?

A. 'Death to all aliens.'

B. 'If it's alien, it's ours.'

C. 'Alien's unite.'

10. What did the Sycorax use to control one third of the human race?

A. Blood.

B. Tea.

C. Radio waves.

11. What is Martha's sister called?

A. Melanie.

B. Tish.

C. Claire.

12. Who were the Daleks ruled by?

A. An Emperor.

B. A President.

C. A Queen.

13. How many Racnoss were born every minute?

A. Seventeen.

B. Four thousand, three hundred and fourty-two.

C. A million.

14. Who did K-9 stay behind with?

A. Rose.

B. Charles Dickens.

C. Sarah Jane.

15. What part of the TARDIS is broken to keep it looking like a Police Box?

A. Disguise circuit.

B. Chameleon circuit.

C. Camoflage circuit.

16. Where was Donna when she suddenly found herself travelling with the Doctor?

A. Her wedding.

B. The cinema.

C. With her mum.

17. What is the twin planet of Raxacoricofallapatorious?

A. The Moon.

B. Krop Tor.

C. Clom.

18. What do the Cybermen want to do to the human race?

A. Destroy them.

B. Upgrade them.

C. Eat them.

19. What was Martha's job when she met the Doctor?

A. Trainee doctor.

B. Shop assistant.

C. Banker.

20. What city did the Doctor and Martha visit on New Earth?

A. New Newcastle.

B. New New York.

C. New New Delhi.

ANSWERS

Complete the quote – Page 3
1. lipstick
2. alone
3. upgrade
4. pest control
5. Moon
6. Gallifrey
7. different

Dalek dash – Page 4
Dalek D will reach the Doctor first.

Judoon jigsaw – Page 5
Pieces A, D and E complete
the picture.

Word wheel – Page 6
The words in the wheel are:
1. Richard Lazarus   6. Witchcraft
2. Slitheen   7. Torchwood
3. Novice Hame   8. Dalek
4. Empress   9. Krillitanes
5. Sylvia Thaw   10. Spider

Sonic Panic – Page 8

Martha's message – Page 9
The message is: Popped out to see
mum. Back in an hour.

TARDIS mix-up – Page 10
A is the real TARDIS.

Who's next? – Page 11
1. D
2. E
3. A
4. C
5. B

Where on Earth are we? – Page 12
A.Egypt, B.New York, C.The Amazon.

Follow that car – Page 14

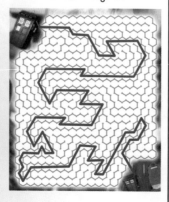

Lost locations – Page 15

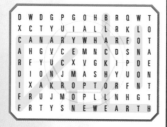

Two of a kind Judoon – Page 16
D and I are the same.

Cyber cancellation code – Page 18

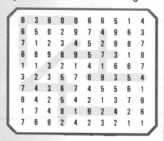

The cancellation code is 6879760.

**Memory game/What can you
remember?** – Page 19/20
1. Five.
2. Red.
3. Four.
4. She's hugging someone.
5. They're in his pockets.

Word grid – Page 21
The related word is TORCHWOOD.

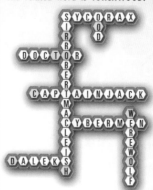

Dodgy Dalek – Page 23
The dodgy Dalek is D.

Family ties – Page 24
A. Tish, B. Leo, C. Mum.

Which bit fits? – Page 25
Bits A, E and F would complete
the picture.

Talk to the Face – Page 26
The message you are left with is:
You are not alone.

Create a code wheel – Page 28
The coded words are Martha, Dalek
and Racnoss.

So many sonics – Page 30
There are 24 sonic screwdrivers.

All in the detail – Page 31
A. Clockwork Robot
B. Dalek
C. Sycorax
D. Cyberman
E. Racnoss

Girl talk – Page 32
Martha said the first quote.
Donna said the second.
Sarah Jane said the third.

To the rescue – Page 33
A is the quickest path for the
Doctor to take.

Doctor whose? – Page 34
The sonic screwdriver, TARDIS,
trainer and psychic paper belong to
the Doctor. The other items do not.

Lost letters – Page 35
The letters spell out Rose.

Alien true or false? – Page 37
1. True.
2. True.
3. True.
4. False. They are interplanetary
police.
5. True.
6. False. It was supposed to make
him younger.
7. True.
8. True.

Carrionite Fright! – Page 38

TARDIS maze – Page 40

**Something Odd about
the Ood** – Page 41
C is the real Ood.

Puzzle pieces – Page 42
Pieces C, E and F would complete
the picture.

Cosmic quiz – Page 44

1. B	8. A	15. B
2. A	9. B	16. A
3. B	10. A	17. C
4. C	11. B	18. B
5. A	12. A	19. A
6. C	13. C	20. B
7. B	14. C	